Mind Your Heart

LIZA MITCHELL R.N.

 FriesenPress

One Printers Way
Altona, MB R0G 0B0
Canada

www.friesenpress.com

Quotes from the Bible are from the New International Version.

ISBN
978-1-03-918969-0 (Hardcover)
978-1-03-918968-3 (Paperback)
978-1-03-918970-6 (eBook)

1. RELIGION, CHRISTIAN LIVING, PERSONAL MEMOIRS

Distributed to the trade by The Ingram Book Company

Dedicated to my precious son.
I miss you, child of my heart.

Mind Your Heart

Foreword

$\mathcal{S}$ ome readers may question the authenticity of my Christian faith upon reading this rendering of a traumatic and somewhat ridiculous time in my life. But I was writing, at the beginning, as I was thinking and acting at that time—not as I should have been. One would think that, being a Christian, I would not have fallen into the kind of behaviour that I am going to describe. But—I fell off the wagon of sense into a big puddle of nonsense.

I write this memoir as a flawed human being who forever will hold onto the conviction that God will be merciful with my failings. There can be times in any of our lives where we fail to follow God's will or leading. But with God's wondrous grace, we can be forgiven.

I did not write this to blame anyone but myself. I did write it to take a realistic look at my questionable behaviour. I needed to look at the things that I had done in that time period that were self-deceiving, selfish, and un-Christlike. I do hope there will be readers that can benefit from my journey back to sanity, and that they will know there is always a way back into God's grace.

Mind Your Heart is written in the form of a memoir of that time in my life.

> "The mind governed by the flesh is death,
> but the mind guided by the Spirit is life and peace."
> – Romans 8:6 (NIV)

I should have remembered that.

Mind Your Heart

My brain
Was aghast
And dark
And turning
With new truth
And clues to
How I had
Finally lost my mind.

The Lost Mind

hat do you do when you have lost your mind? Do you go looking for it? Where? In your underwear drawer? In the bottom of the sea? In the opinion of someone else? No, not that particular opinion—the one that says, "You have lost it!" (*Yes, I have*); "You are crazy!" (*That helps—really*); "What is wrong with you?" (*If I knew, I would have fixed it*). I would not have been listening to Sean say these things had I not actually lost my mind in the first place.

Self-humiliation fills me right now. Self-humiliation comes immediately after one shows absurd behaviour in the view of a loved one. It also leads to the sickest feeling in the lowest pit of my stomach. I cannot erase any of it, no matter what the cause. Plus, nothing I could say or scream or cry or beg or think could take away what I had done. I was guilty as charged, now locked away from his presence for life, sentenced to a forever of regret. (Or maybe a bit less, with good behaviour, or self-forgiveness—one can hope.)

Those first seemingly endless days after the incident, I kept thinking, *end it all*. How can you face anyone knowing you have been a fool of the greatest proportion, and that you cannot even figure out a good reason for it? How can you face people, thinking that they can see the shame in you, thinking that they will look at you like they do when they believe a person is mentally imbalanced? Or see you as somewhat off, someone never to get close to? How was I going to survive this, feeling like I had felt all my life—the odd one out, the one people preferred to keep at a distance, the one who was not like anyone else? Better off to leave this life and avoid all the future humiliation and embarrassment. And most of all, to get away from this mind of mine that got lost, but is now back with a vengeance of self-loathing and guilt.

Of course, ending it was not really a choice. It would be an escape for me, but a prison of grief for those who did love me. I pondered it in those hours after what I did, but I knew it was the worst way to avoid the consequences of what I had done. And was what I had done worth that much sorrow? Was his opinion worth anything anyway?

How did I get to this place in life? And why?

Well, I'll get to that, and to what I did after I lost my mind, later.

A Few Days After
I Lost My Mind

I'm doing better as the endless minutes of the days go by. I worked—I looked normal. I smiled when I should have, laughed a bit, concentrated on what was more important than my feelings. I told myself not to think about the almost-panic-attack I had in the car on the way into work. *Do not think of him—it has to be final.* I will put the *block* method in place. My sister had told me about this block method years earlier. As soon as an unwelcome or inappropriate thought comes into your brain, think, *block*, somewhat like stamping the thought with a *No Smoking* sign—without the cigarette, of course. What is stamped *blocked* is not to be looked at or thought about.

Keep busy during your week off—I will.

I have my dream job now. It came so late in life and now seems about to disappear. Lately, I feel like everything is about to disappear. Job, house, my sanity, now him. It seems if I love something right now, it's going to disappear. And I am feeling far from God. How can He look at me? I hate looking at myself. All I see is ugly age, and eyes that will always be guilty. And what about forgiveness? Sean will forgive me, even though he sees me as so flawed. That's quite unlike the picture of himself that he presented to me. Yes, he will forgive, and that will make him feel noble. But he will never forget my transgressions. He has, many times in the past, liked to remind me of former failings and minor mistakes.

I wonder if he is cursed with the inability to forget. Maybe he cannot help himself. We have been broken up three times now, and I assume that he thinks it has always been all my fault. If I am that faulty, why did he get back with me the second and third times? A good question, which will never be answered. He is the master of not giving a straight or concrete answer about any of our personal stuff. He thinks that I do not notice. He can quote the Bible easily in full chapters. He remembers so much of history, especially that of Scotland. He annoyingly gets all therapist-like sometimes, as he said he used to be one. But for anything personal about us, especially when it concerns *planning*— there are no clear or concrete answers.

I will not paint him totally with a bad brush—what happened that night was all my fault. Not everything in the past sixteen months had been, however. He was definitely guilty of making the relationship difficult. But that night had been my fault. I wonder if he is at home burning holes in the top I left behind—evidence. Not likely—I imagine the garbage can has my top right now. The last traces of me in his house lying in the dark, piled with malodorous refuse and old paper and plastic. Long forgotten, never understood. I have his shirt. I washed it. I cannot give it back to him, as there is no way to do that. No one can know what I did, so there is no one to ask to return it to him. My son and the friends I was with that night know, but they forgive and also volunteer to lie for me if needed. I expected that from my son, appreciated it from the others. (Yes, I know it is not acceptable to lie.)

But now, the one who used to say he loved me has become a victim of my behaviour. I will never know if he will forgive me.

Now, to go back to where it really started. *Oh my.*

Playing

He plays at love
He plays at life
He plays his guitar
Like it is a knife
Sharp and sure
To cut my heart
Let it bleed
Not noticed at all
Because
He's playing at life.

I stand alone
Within his sight
He plays his guitar
Like it is a fight
Against my love
He lets it drown
In indifference
Because
He's playing at life.

I'd give him love
I'd give him all
But he plays his guitar
Like it is his call
To see me gone
For always and forever
Because
He's playing at life.

The Crush

Where do I begin? Oh yes, a church pew, about five years previous to this mind-losing incident. Innocent enough, you say—maybe so. There, or at singing practice—I cannot recall which—the crush started the minute I saw Sean for the first time. Then, for three years following that, I crushed on him—not in any inappropriate way, as I did not want to think of him in an unchristian-like manner. I loved his looks, his quietness mixed with his exuberance when singing praise songs, his silly jokes. If there is such a thing as an aura, his attracted me strongly. I never figured that I would have a chance to be with him, as he was younger, as he never seemed to notice me, and, worse, if we did speak, I always walked away feeling embarrassed. I was so nervous when I spoke with him that I babbled on like a teenager. And the crush had to be enough then, as I had not been too bright of a bulb in my relationships before.

I must interject here that I did have a long first marriage, and that relationship is in no way included in my relationship mistakes.

God had told me to stay away from men after my second divorce from a short nightmare of a marriage. I only needed Him, and I had listened to Him for five years. No dates, no relationships, nothing for five solid years. And actually, I had been happy that way.

During those years I was without a man in my life, I had felt free. Free from not being in love with a man. Free from worrying about being lied to, being cheated on. Free from hoping I was still good-looking enough, free from basing my worth on a man's opinion. Alone. Single. Chaste. Some people might find that kind of life abhorrent, pitiable, or boring. I had been free to be busy with whatever I had wanted to do, and not subject to any man's schedule or idiosyncrasies. I'd had enough of that.

I never should have looked at Sean. My freedom was gone. My days of yearning for a man to be in my company were back. Distracting thoughts, silly thoughts, enslaving thoughts were on their way back. And then, attaching myself to someone like Sean, I found out it was like trying to hold onto a greased pig. You got just enough of a touch to feel him, then, *whoosh*, he was out of your grasp.

It might have been God working. It might have been circumstances intertwining. It might only have been human happenstance, but we started to text when my son was seriously ill and in the hospital. He had come to visit my son but said he could not get in to see him, so he texted me. One text leading to more type-talking, we both admitted (*Or was it just me? No, it was him, too*) that we had liked each other for quite a while. Oh, those days, it was just a crush. Before the crush turning into liking. Before the liking turned to love. *Before the love turned to obsession?*

Could I say that? Did I believe that? Was I obsessed? At the beginning, I gave no thought to obsession. I had no idea it would rear its ugly head. I know for sure that I had just loved him too much—more than he truthfully deserved.

I liked the feeling I got when I was with him, when I looked at him. That *I am smiling with a sunny warmth on the inside* feeling. He was so sweet. He seemed tentative about trying to get physically close to me at first. But I could tell he wanted to. And I wanted him to. It is very sad that a relationship can start out so sweet and light, but later, become sour and dark. At the beginning, you think you are seeing clearly in that light, but later you discover that darkness can settle in.

Were our personalities too different? Yes, but there were many things that we had in common, so I ignored the differences. The differences should have been the first warning sign or red flag that I acknowledged. I did see warning signs, but I tend to talk myself out of them, reason them away. Did I not want to see faults or incompatibilities? Likely not, as I had reasoned similar things away in the past. But reasoning things away or thinking they will change because you wish it so does not change a thing. It just leaves you on edge, always waiting for things that are never going to happen. Men should be blunter. Don't say, "Be patient, honey." *No.* Say, "Never going to happen, woman." That might make a woman stop lingering, waiting for the never-to-be.

And wait I did, at first, as it started out fairly normally. We did things like hike and go to his secret wildflower sources, but within a few months, it all came down to sitting with him in church on the Sunday mornings our group was leading worship, a few hours at my house Sunday afternoon, then back to his life I never really knew that much about. Oh, but of course, he always told me the reasons why he had little time for me—his family obligations, his work, his need to be alone. But I wanted more time.

So, there my mind went into another mistake. The first mistake: ignoring the warning signs; now this second mistake: letting myself feel rejected. Why do some of us women let ourselves feel rejected, as if it is all to do with our worth? I found out pretty quickly that I disliked feeling rejected by him. It made me feel angry—not crazy angry, just that slow, simmering feeling of resentment under the skin. But I should have known: add a little more heat and the simmer can turn into a boil.

Especially when it came to his birthday.

Sean said he did not celebrate his birthdays. I thought he was kidding. I bought him a gift I knew he would love, the absolutely perfect card. I asked him what kind of cake he wanted, only to be firmly told, "No birthday!" So, the cake never got baked, his gift I gave to my son, the perfect card was ripped up, and we broke up. In my head, it came down to *I am not important enough to celebrate his birthday with him.* I imagined him celebrating with his family—but me, I was left on the outside. That should have been a big-time clue. The red flag was waving again.

So, you see mistake number three: I was trying to please a man that did not want to be pleased. At least not by me.

Well, the worst mistake, which helped the first breakup along before the birthday debacle, was talking to his older children. They said so many awful things about him that the world of him in my brain was swirling around in a dizzying mixture of what I believed to be true, what they said was true, and wondering what was true. I knew about his past, so that was not a surprise. But was he not the man now that he had presented to me from the beginning? I loved him. I planned a conversation—yes, *planned*—even the happy, agreeable ending. I imagined he would see my side of it; he would say, "Oh yes, I need to change that." Nothing went as I had planned. He denied everything that I had been told. I was confused, plus guilty of inappropriate listening. Nothing was settled.

The more I think and write, the more I see what I did wrong. But I did a lot of things right as well. He was not innocent. Yet I just cannot totally talk badly about a man I could possibly still love. Wait-brain is off, block-Sean mode is on. Because love is not in the cards anymore. I have to accept that. I feel like he sees me as a waste of time. I refuse to cry.

I digress again.

Liking

What do, and did, I like about him? This is a compilation of past, present, and, obviously, no future. He loves Jesus, he is musically talented, he is super intelligent, he likes Scottish history, he looks unbelievably good in a kilt, he could calm me, he loves his family, he is witty, he's a great kisser and lover, he smells good, he is witty and always made me laugh, he loves *Outlander*, he loves cats, cats love him, he loves animals, he is gentle. (Thinking of his gentleness reminds me of the time he delicately took a butterfly out of a spider's web.) When I was with him, I was more into the Word, and we would discuss scripture and then I would delve further into whatever subject we had been discussing. In some ways, he made me better, but I allowed other parts of our relationship to make me a lesser and much worse person.

Well, there my mind was going, back to my tendency to like being with a man; that feeling that makes my spirit feel young and new again. That pre-love period where all is good and simple and kind and sugar-sweet—the period before the fall into love.

Loving should be easy.

We got back together a few months later. I fell madly back into him the moment I saw him in his kilt at the

Highland Games. I saw this irresistible glow around him. I was blinded by the wrong light. He gave me a big hug. His hugs always made me feel I was being welcomed into a safe, warm place. Sitting together at the annual Music Fest a month and a half later while he gently rubbed my leg, we appreciated the music and atmosphere. I was back in; we would be okay this time. Happiness tinged with fear. I wanted it to turn out differently this time. I would be different. Maybe he would be different. But the definition of insanity I have heard was true: Doing the same thing all over again and expecting the outcome to be different.

Obviously, I had forgotten how we had ended the first time. Why would I consider going back to someone who had talked to me like that? He was text-arguing with me just before my shift in the city. I always had to say something back. It ended with him saying, in reply to my question of why he had started seeing me in the first place, that it was because he had *thought* I was a good Christian woman. Yes, he had declared I was a heathen. Nothing worse could be said about me. He had also said he was going to be happier without me; that being alone was better than being with me. I was crying by the time I got to work, embarrassed, as one of the nurses had seen me. But I stopped and held my sorrow in for twelve hours, then cried all the way home during the forty-five-minute drive.

Big mistake number five was now on its way, as we got back together for the second time. I thought that I would be able to expect less and be okay with less.

But we resumed for the second time, nonetheless. Maybe we are both a bit crazy. Maybe it's not just me.

I Wish

I wish we could dance in the rain
Then lie together under the stars
Sharing heartbeats and sighs
Under a tent cover of love.

I wish we could float in time
Surfacing only to take a breath
Making love until we sleep
Dreaming of what's yet to come.

I wish we'd love forever into Heaven
Carried on wings we share in faith
Flying softly to a Home
With no end to our love.

Loving

*F*alling in love, for me personally, is equal to letting go of sense, letting go of clear sight, letting go of sanity. Yes, that is what I do when I fall headfirst into what I think is a true state of love. I had promised myself, for those previously mentioned five years, that I would never allow that again. I was not a smart woman with men. I had failed too many times, done too many stupid things, imagined lies to be the truth—mostly the lies to myself. Was I really going to do this again? Was I crazy? Well, that is the question on the table right now, is it not?

I had fallen easily in love with him, not even thinking about it at all. I was so used to liking him that loving seemed the natural progression of things. He said he loved me many times. I do not know if I believed him. I have never felt lovable in that way. Perhaps that is why I am such a pleaser. My children call that being a doormat. However, Sean was not a man to use anyone as a doormat. He just had what I called his "rules."

We were back together the second time, and it was all good at first. He said he would try to spend more time with me during the week, and he did—at the beginning. Then it was every second week. There were too many things that he had to do instead of seeing me—like having a bonfire alone, riding horses in the rain (well, that could have been made up). Even so, made up or not, the latter does sound more fun than being in my company. And I must insert here that I saw little of him on the weekends. That is a whole other future story. So—was I too clingy, was I too needy? Is it not just normal to want to be in the close vicinity of someone you love?

But let's get back to what I called his rules. He did not like me cooking for him—that was "imposing," he said. He did not like me giving him anything—that might be fair. No planning. No giving advice. No talking about holidays. No using my shampoo or toothpaste when he showered here after work on one of the few nights he would see me during the week—that was also "imposing." I mention this minor thing only because in my after-the-second-breakup I-need-to-get-over-Sean journal (which was later burned when I imagined I was over him), I had written, *He will use my body but not my shampoo.* Yes, as my mother always told me, I am "saucy." I resented his rules, as I saw them as controlling everything in the relationship. I felt he was invalidating me for who I was.

Our last evening together started a bit "off." We were eating, and he began listing all of the stressful issues in his life—something I was usually empathetic about. But that evening we were supposed to be discussing reaching common ground, not just all about him. I could see by this opening that it was not going to be about what I wanted at all. I started to cry. He yelled at me—something he had never done before. The rest of the evening was good, except I could see there was no common ground reached except in his eyes. His way *only*—maybe that's why it all ended up on the highway again.

So, it disintegrated again, very quickly. I wanted more time with him; he thought his estimate was correct. I got resentful—especially about the weekends. The texting back and forth was awful again, probably with both of us taking things the wrong way. I thought I was being helpful, sympathetic, stating my case. But my case got closed and we broke up again.

It was worse for me that time than before. I felt guilt, some anger, and also kept wondering who was right or wrong. It soon turned into depression and anxiety. My daughter saw I was in a very bad place, so she got me in to see a counsellor. I eventually felt sane again. Five months went by. I felt good. I felt over him. I was ready to go back to church; ready to go back to singing with the group.

Then the virus came, and we all had to stay home.

Leaking

Heartache, heartbreak,
Nothing left to feel
But cold and alone
With my love leaking
Slowly into nowhere.

What?

*J*ust a month or two before the shutdown, he had sent a reply to me on a group email and we had started talking a bit. Yes, he started it the third time, not me, as he so nicely accused me of later. Then, thinking I was ready to be cool and distant, I volunteered to help him with his house reno. Yes, this was the first minor break in my soon-to-be lost sanity. Obviously, I was not thinking sensibly. Was I thinking I wanted to start a relationship again? Maybe I did—*bad idea*. I guess I should have remembered that definition of insanity. Maybe I should have bought a fridge magnet.

I told myself I'd be better this time—cool and detached. I would not want a relationship with him. I would just be his friend. I had been on a dating website and had considered trying again. But I'd think of Sean and hesitate. Alas, lucky for me—not for others, obviously—the virus stopped all that. Dating was now a forbidden act, something that would have to be clandestine. No one would take that chance on an individual they had no history with except a few lines of chat on a computer. I felt relieved and went off the site. *Clue in here, girl. Why do you never guard your heart? Or, better yet, use your brain?*

I went to his house twice. The first time, I was so nervous, I made myself sick. Waiting for my snow tires to be taken off, I was in and out of the bathroom, hoping no one would notice and think I should be avoided. If only they could have seen into my future.

The second time at his place was better—not so nervous.

I was smiling again. Not good.

Sliding into a Bad Place

*W*hat started my quick slide back into that familiar bad place in my mind was a text. Simple? No. I had mentioned to him, jokingly, in my text back to him, that my son had accused me of drunk-texting him. I do not remember why he had said that. I'm unlikely to be drunk-texting, as I have a limited capacity for alcohol. Then a text came back from Sean listing four things he hated being accused of, things he obviously was saying that I had accused him of in the past. *Excuse me?* This seemed like a dig. A dig meant to make me feel bad . . . or guilty? A dig meant to hurt me, already only having been back together for a week? Well, buddy, hit me with the whole shovel if you want to hurt me. Don't send just a dig that you can later say was not meant to hurt. A shovel, honey . . . that makes it nice and clear.

Then—the weekend. Here I go. He did not have his kids because of the virus, so I thought, even if he had to be in town at his parents', he'd be able to come over to my place for a bit. *Nope.* I was to go for a short drive on Sunday afternoon before he had to make supper for his parents (if he actually did do that). *Really??* Is that all I was worth to him, a few minutes on a Sunday afternoon?

Okay, so here, now, is a critical question: Was I being selfish? I felt he was being a jerk. What was it about weekends with him? This is where I am not sure what was or what was not reality. What was I not seeing or realizing? (I think I was realizing something, but it was something I just did not want to face.) I sent him a text—I never have figured out why we hardly ever spoke on the phone—and told him goodbye. I regretted it a bit as soon as I sent it, but it was history repeating itself again. Fucking weekends. *Fuck him!*

I thought I was okay with this breakup. It had not been that long this time. The last breakup period had been for five months, at which time I had felt I was over him, over letting my mind drive me. Seemingly, I was not.

So, that same evening, I felt recklessly free and decided to just get over him and get on with it. So, my son, his friend, and I randomly ended up having a "how-to-roll-joints" session. Yes, I know, weird, and so very random. But then, I do have a history of doing iffy things when I am restless or at odds with myself.

I failed the class, but decided to sample my failed creation. I had not smoked pot in many years, but I remembered liking it. So there it was. The pot exaggerated that feeling of rejection I had always hated. My mind started going in a senseless direction.

Did the pot make me lose all sense? It didn't help, I am sure. Sean hated pot, even though he said he had never tried it. When the final reckoning occurred, I could not admit that I had been high. I could not tell him that. He'd say . . . you know, I really do not know what he would have said. Maybe it would have just added to his other comments: "Are you crazy?", "What is wrong with you?", "You are acting like a criminal," "Have you lost your mind?", "You are a stalker,"

"You are obsessed." All in the calm, mature voice of the one who knows at that moment that he has the upper hand. Because of what I had done, I felt that I would never get out from under it. I would remain the lower being in his eyes, and always in my own. And in God's eyes.

I wished I could hide.

Trying to Hide

I decided I should hide. Work my two scheduled shifts, then hide. But first, right after the insane behaviour, I partied all night at the neighbour's place. Nothing bad—playing Taboo, and karaoke with my son's friends. It was unusual for me to be over there, where my son most often went alone, but I had to lose myself in something. More pot, a drink, lots of laughing and singing. No outward condemnation, even though I deserved it. The night just went on, and I tried to pretend I had not screwed up. Hoping at some point he would show up at the door and scream at me, shame me, condemn me with his eyes. Wondering if he would really send the police after me. But no, he would sleep in his peace, feeling the rightness of the victim, forgetting me in a few moments. I deserved punishment. But Sean knew the best punishment for me was to be cut off from him. He would again get to wallow in his self-righteousness—but this time, he would have just cause.

I hid, avoiding contact with as many people as I could. I could not face my shame. If he told his mother, I would never be able to return to my church. Ironic, as I had stayed away already for five months, so I could get over him. So, I blocked emails from anyone I knew from church. I would pretend to have disappeared when church was allowed to resume. I could not go back to the singing group. I had just told the leader I would. Now, again, I had screwed up, and could not go back. What could I give as a reason, when I could not say what I had done? Humiliating. Better to pretend I was gone from sight. Better to remain a mystery.

I also would not go to the grocery store on the weekends. Best not to risk running into him or his mother. Although . . . wearing a mask might help. All technical methods of communication with him have been blocked, even emailing. I cannot have any trace of thinking that I would see or hear from him again. It had to be over and done. Sean was not good for me, and I was definitely not good for him. The finality was actually helping me cope. It is easier to deal with reality when you know circumstances can never change.

Confession

I should start with some background.

I always had in my mind that, yes, he was at his parents' every weekend. But that after he took his kids home on Saturday evening, he would go back to his place in the city. I was assuming he was lying to me when he said he always went back to his parents' house. That is what he had always told me he did. I wanted to know for sure. Over time, whether we were together or not, this became for me a source of discontent and irritation. Whenever the weekends were brought up, whether in a peaceful way or a contentious way, I never felt the issue had any resolution. I knew that he lied at times, so I assumed he was lying to me about this, especially since the reasons for him not being able to see me on the weekends often changed. And he always was vague. I like details and things black-and-white, so his vagueness and varied explanations were not enough for me.

Yes, I have read the book *He's Just Not That Into You*. I know what the male author said: men will always make time for what is important to them. So, I was not that important to him. I hated feeling that. But he stuck to his version of the truth, and I to mine.

I will never know for certain the entire truth about any of the weekends. I only can attest to the truth about that last weekend that I had been wrong—so very wrong! And so very insane.

In my high mind, I convinced myself that I had to prove that I was right—he was lying about his whereabouts. I was going to catch him in his lies. I would finally discover what the truth was. Yes, I would finally prove it. Had I been thinking sanely, I would have remembered that this was only one weekend, not all of them. Proving he was or was not at his parent's was not indicative of where he was all those other weekends. But my thinking was irrational, and I was stoned.

Thinking I was being all tough, I called him and stated I needed to see him in person, *like now*. He said he could meet me in his truck outside his parents' house for a few minutes. Since I thought he was not there and really did not mean it, I said no, I wanted him at my place. Had I had any common sense at the time, I would have just gone over there. But I thought he was just pretending and knew that I would not come over. Somehow, he ended up hanging up on me. Well, no wonder.

I then sent him a text saying I would just call him on his mother's phone, something I would never have done—even in the state I was in. But I continued further on down the path to craziness.

After no reply, I texted him that I was on my way to his place. Stupid, in a way, because if he was really there, he could just leave temporarily and make it look like he was not there in the first place. But my mind just let me continue on, descending into worse behaviour.

I left for his place, a forty-minute drive. Yes, I know—a stupid, insane thing to do. Even the most idiotic person in the world would know that. What had I been thinking? If I was correct and caught him at home, he would certainly not put out a welcome mat. He would be pissed and angry. I would have no recourse but to flee in shame. He also could say that he had just driven there from his parents'. Not likely, as I drive way faster than he does. But my die was cast and I did not turn back. I continued thinking I was going to settle something. *Yes, something got settled, alright.*

When I got there, he was not at home. Then, a faint ray of reality started to settle in, but not bright enough to make me turn around and just go back home. I should have realized that I had some sensible choices to make at that moment. Like a carousel, the choices we can make go around and around in our heads, and we grab the best choice, most of the time. But my carousel was spinning too fast. I turned away from the good choices. I went inside—the door was unlocked. I decided I would stay, clean up the kitchen (it was still a mess from our dinner two nights before), smoke some more, and then sleep until he came home. *Duh!* I gave his cat some affection and conversation and went to find a shirt to change into while I cleaned up the kitchen. I took off my top and put one of his shirts on, leaving the top on the chair in the TV room. The shirt smelled of cigarettes, but it was his shirt, so I ignored the smoky odour.

Then my phone rang. *Oh, boy*—it was Sean wanting to know when I was coming over to his parents' house. He had misinterpreted my text. He said he had told his parents and that the house was on "high alert" since I had "threatened them" and I was a "stalker." This was a lie, as I had not said I was going over there. I told him that I had meant his house in the city. Then he asked if I had gone crazy. I answered, "I guess I have." What else was I supposed to say? Then he said that if I had broken into his house (the door was open), he was going to call the police. That what I had done was criminal. I told him to go ahead. He asked me what I had done to his house. He was continuing on as if he was talking to a real-life stalker and violent person. Did he not know me? Or was this so he could feel even more self-righteous? Was his mother listening, and he wanted to make me sound really insane and threatening? Or was I really like that kind of person?

I grabbed my stuff and left immediately. During this, he was on the phone saying all the kind of things an insane person really wants to hear: "What is wrong with you?", "Are you insane?", "You have lost it!", "You are obsessed!", "You need help," "I am going to change my locks," the police again. I had no answers for him except, "Do you want my licence plate number? I'll give it to you now." What could I say? I was acting crazy. I was out of my mind. I was wrong— so embarrassingly, humiliatingly wrong. I was acting like an obsessed stalker at the time. Did it mean that I had always been obsessed with him? That night might have been a clue to the truth about myself.

Interlude

*Y*ou, Sean, are a lovely man; but Sean, you are still an emotional deserter. Once there is any sign you have to show your true self, you run. You retreat. You hide. No bravery. What do you fear? Rejection? Being known?

I know you have a beautiful soul in there somewhere, but it's covered in layers of hidden truths and overt lies. Anything to cover you up, blanket over your head, hoping no one will see you. Sean, I see you. I see with filmy eyes the *you* in there I want to love. The *you* that just wants to be held in arms of eternal trust; arms that will never fail you; arms that see you as forgiven, bought with the blood of Christ.

But you will never believe that my arms could be any part of that trust. You see my flaws, you examine my thoughts, you fight my heart. You don't want me to love you. Loving you would mean that I approve of you, and you cannot take into yourself something I think you have never felt before. That does not mean you were never given approval; it just means you never felt it. All the other negativity in your life was drowning out the positive stuff.

Where is that part of you, that part of us, that is unreachable? Is it in the brain? It likely is. Or is it in the heart—the heart that makes the brain suffer? We feel all the ache of suffering in our chest, the physical heart, but the pain is really in our brains. So maybe a sign on a psychologist's door should say, "If you are planning on following your heart, turn around."

I could have loved you had you been more willing. Or I less demanding. Is it really demanding when we ask with love in mind? Where does the line get drawn? And who gets to draw the line in the first place? But we were two parallel lines that would never meet.

I have had the thought that absolute lust can often give the same feeling as real love. The lines cross. But there is no trust in lust. And no happy ending. The fire can burn for only so long. One person will drift off with the smoke, floating away slowly

from the origin of the heat. No trace left of any truth. Was the truth here, Sean, that you felt only lust for me? Or not enough of lust or love to want to be with me more?

And real love—I cannot describe what I have never felt from anyone except a late, beloved male friend. But I know what it is to really love someone else, so I can describe that.

If I love you, I never want to make you feel badly, even if you should. You need to know that no matter what happens or what you do, I would be there 100 percent for you. I would make you feel approved of, encouraged, seen. I would do that in so many, many ways. Other than God, you would be the most important person in my life. However, you would never require me to neglect my children or family for you. You would know my love is forever.

But alas, Sean, you do not want that kind of love. You seem to view that type of love as abnormal, a hint of psychological trouble. You want a woman who does not need you, a woman who will be satisfied with hardly seeing you, a woman who cannot outwardly show love for you. You said things like *love* and *soulmate* to me, but you acted like what you wanted was to be an occasional lover, a friend with benefits, a booty call. You made promises, talked of the future, but it was a future that never came to be. When with me, you were what I thought you really were, but apart, you were someone else. You did not need a woman like me. You needed a cold-hearted woman. That might have suited you better. Yes, listen to the anger that was there that I had always denied.

But why do I fuss over this all still? I should have clued in way sooner than I did.

Undone

My hand is in yours
But you won't feel it.
My heart beats close
But you won't hear it.
We meet lips
And bodies
Yet
Your soul won't touch mine.

My face is in your eyes
But you don't see it.
My thought is in your mind
But you don't think it.
We breathe air
And heat
Yet
You don't inhale it.

My love is in your hands
But you won't hold tight.
My voice is in your ears
But you won't hear it.
We hear music
And notes
Yet
You leave the song unsung.

Panic in the Aftermath

*D*riving home from his house, my mind was a whirl. *What had I done? Had I actually been wrong about what he did on the weekends? Was he lying about them or not? Was I unreasonable? Was I really obsessed? Why had I lost it? What was wrong with me? Please, God, no police. I could lose my nursing license. Would he have been happy if the worst had happened to me? Would he gloat if he had me in jail? Was he really that mean?*

But I had to concentrate on my driving. *Do not speed. Remember your old driving routes from his place to yours.* It was dark. I had to be careful.

As I drove, I could smell cigarettes. What? Then I remembered I still had his shirt on and had left my top behind. Oh, boy. He would eventually see my top on the chair and wonder what the nutty woman had worn on her car ride home. And why she had taken her top off in the first place.

I got home alright—obviously, as I was not in jail or worse. He never called the police. I was not arrested. I was guilty, but not to be punished by the law. But my mind and heart were punished. I made myself feel numb. I told myself it was for the best—what a stupidly overused expression. *Whose* best? And who gets to say what is best? Yes, I know: God.

I could not talk to God about what I had done. He knows all, so obviously, He saw all that I thought and did. It made no sense that I felt so disconnected from God, except that, in this state of pure shame, I could not face Him. I knew God forgives us when we confess our sins to Him. But I felt I did not deserve forgiveness. And although God's grace is free and abundant, I could not seem to take it, as I felt too loathsome a human being.

God gives us this life to learn, to reach higher spiritual knowledge, to prepare us for spiritual perfection in Heaven. He gives us many life situations to teach us lessons, to show His love and grace. But I always seem to need to learn the hard way. This lesson was one of the hardest to hit me. And I am still not sure what God was trying to show me, teach me—except maybe stay away from men who will not (or cannot) love me. Or, stay away from men altogether.

Without knowing the truth on both sides, I will never be able to ascertain how much of all of this was my fault. Could any of this be his fault? I did all the crazy actions—so it was all my fault that night. I had tolerated his behaviour. I l had let him drive me bonkers. I had let the lies and stories go. I went back with him, knowing he was never going to change and could still be drinking. He always had said, "It's just me. I don't change." So many times, he said that. I should have listened and really heard him.

It's a very old misconception that so many women still believe, that our love will change a man. That if we love them enough, do enough for them, sacrifice enough for them, forgive them enough, they will fall madly in love with us. And yes, I know, the millennials would laugh into their eight-dollar lattes at reading such madness.

What was wrong with me? I had tried to get that out of the counsellor that I had seen after the second breakup. No counsellor will ever answer that question. Cognitive behavioural therapy never addresses that. *No, we are to change the way we think about ourselves, find out what is right about us. Change our thoughts to change our behaviour.*

Obviously, my sessions had only worked temporarily. And again, it was God's way I should have been taking. But I had steered in the wrong direction. I went the route of thinking it was God's will that I was with Sean, that He had plans for us, that He wanted us together for a reason. Oh, how the nonspiritual part of our brain can deceive us—the part that Satan gets to so easily. He plays on our weaknesses, knows what temptations we most easily give into. No, I am not saying the devil made me do it. I made my choices. I did not listen to God. I was weak. I did not seek God's strength and truth. I sought truths that were never going to reveal themselves, no matter what I said or did or imagined.

I needed to learn to give up. Or better, listen to God.

You

One thought of you and the sun shines
It scorches my heart and my body wins
The prize of your face near mine
Breathe love on me
Always forever be
The place where love begins.

Take me, shape me into the mold of your skin
Touch me, blend me with your soul within
Run your fingers through my thoughts
Caress the sky
Inside my thighs
As I slowly take you in.

Preciously linger with no ending in mind
Bodies, thoughts, all forever entwined
Kiss me, touch me, as only you do
Making me yours
Forever.

Your Touch

Your touch floats me softly
Into the warmth that is you
And with your kiss, you seep
Cell by cell, into me
Until I am filled
With nothing but longing
To be drifting away
On the sea of your pleasure
As you caress
The deepest parts
Of the one
Who was me
But now who
Becomes softly part of you.

Lost Love

You can see from my poetry that I am a hopeless romantic. Sometimes that's not a good thing as it allows me to revel in feelings rather than sense. Heart over brain. The Bible says the heart is deceitful—yes, it is. I let my heart believe that I needed Sean more than I needed my sanity.

I was out for a walk today and I had a moment of angst thinking of Sean. My deceitful heart, for a moment, was missing him. It soon passed. Brain wins, for once. I had an old male acquaintance over the evening before, and we had had an innocent evening of talking and laughing. My son had given me the look again. I could feel his objections, as he thinks I never have any sense when it comes to men. He's correct. I have to prove him wrong—or maybe myself. I felt guilty seeing this friend from the past, but I also knew there was no reason to feel guilty. Sean and I were done. I knew that.

I love my long walks with my music and my thoughts. I still question if I should go back to my church, back to the group. Will he make a remark in front of the group? Will his mother gossip about my behaviour in church? I felt the answer to both these questions was *no*, as he revels in his silence and I knew his mother was not a gossip. Yet I feared anyway that the unforeseen would happen, and I would have to flee in red-faced embarrassment. As you can see, I am good at imagining dramatic scenarios in my mind.

I think some of us females have watched too many romantic movies. I detest those love movies that come on at Christmas or other celebratory occasions. They make me gag. But still, the false view of romance lives in me. The kind that imagines a man recognizing, after a breakup, that he really cannot live without you. He braves the elements and time to hurry to your side to express his undying and eternal love. Sean is definitely not one of those men. He would rather make the point he does not need me at all. He can do without me. I am not worth chasing after.

Who, then, is braver? Sean, who stays inside himself and never makes a move? Or me, who tries to give my all and then, too much, knowing deep in my heart (or brain) that it will never matter to him how much I try?

Someone told me many years ago: Liza, you cannot make someone love you. That has proven always to be true.

My grandmother told me when I was in my early twenties, "Men are like buses—if you miss one, another one will be along in ten minutes." I should have listened and waited the ten minutes.

Sean is lost to me, along with whatever love I had hoped or imagined could exist between us. However, I have come to terms with the cold fact that I never really had him anyway, and likely never would have. His mind was not for the having. He was a bus that was never going to open his door for me, let alone accept my bus pass. He was one of those buses with a "Not Going Anywhere With Liza" sign lit up.

Talk about more loss—my position at my dream job will end soon. I am so disappointed, but reality again has to be faced. I love this job and will miss it. Being resilient, I will survive having to go back to community nursing. Knowing that my temporary position was a gift that God favoured me with so late in life, I cannot choose anything but to be grateful, even if it was short-lived.

Worry or Concern

*M*atthew 6:34 says, "Therefore do not worry about tomorrow, for tomorrow will worry about itself. Each day has enough trouble of its own." Sean had once said we are not to worry—we are to be *concerned*, but not to worry.

Well, I am sincerely concerned that my recent actions will increase the stain that sin leaves on my soul. I know my sins are forgiven, the stains washed away by Christ's blood, but I still feel the guilt and the feeling of stains remaining on the white robe that is promised to us by Jesus. I do well for a while, then I screw up again. Maybe we all do in one way or another. But if what I did is too embarrassing to tell most people, then I can assume it's in the major category. I have been a Christian for forty years, so this type of screwup should not belong in my life.

I am not too fond of myself lately. I feel I should be more like other Christian women. But that has never been me. So, I do not feel like I fit into most circles. I can act like I do, but I do not feel it. I am good at my job, but then I question the reason why I did not get hired by the new employer. I am sad about that, but I will not let that show until the first second of my final walk out the door. I have been able to hide any feelings I still might have for Sean. At least, I have convinced myself of that.

Actually, most times, I feel empty or numb, maybe indifferent to my past feelings. What is useless has to be put out of mind and heart. *Suck it up*, as my bestie says. Buck up. Get over it and get on with it. *C'est la vie, mon ami.*

Heartbreak

"Above all else, guard your heart,
for everything you do flows from it."
– Proverbs 4:23

"Trust in the Lord with all your heart
and lean not on your own understanding."
– Proverbs 3:5

What does it feel like when your heart is broken? Not the heartbreak experienced from losing a child or other family member; not the heartbreak of losing your health, or job, or home. I mean the broken heart that happens when love ends and the sorrow of it is so severe you feel that nothing will ever heal the wound. Medically, it has been proven that people can die of a broken heart, so there are physical effects. And, of course, many emotional effects as well.

To me, the pain of heartbreak is akin to opening a new, raw wound with every breath taken in and out; an ache in your chest that never goes away; a sharp stab with every memory that gets through the sorrow; a melody that can never be sung again. If one is lucky, it can be a sad, empty numbness. No arms can heal the break, no kiss can wipe it away.

No man has ever really broken my heart. I have had God to heal any wounds in those types of situations. Plus, no human would have that power over me. I feel, since all this with Sean, something has happened to my heart. It feels bruised and defeated. I let him into my heart and I should not have done it. I trusted my own judgment, which has very often been skewed, letting my infatuation with him blind me to basic common sense. I had never thought I would let this happen again. As he was a Christian, I assumed that all would go well. But nothing human holds any guarantee.

But it's not his fault. I believe, now, that I broke my own heart.

And I will let it stay that way. Broken and silent, numb and empty. I do feel numb these days. I just keep going, doing what I am supposed to do, working until the job ends, hoping nothing worse happens.

With the virus, it seemed as if the world might become quiet, with people too busy being isolated to cause trouble. But sin and evil continue, as they will until the end— crashes, shootings, murders, robberies, police brutality, riots. And the never-ending news-watching. And the insane weather occurrences. "Birth pangs" have started, as spoken of in the Bible, referring to catastrophic weather happening near the end of time.

Life Goes On

I have not gotten into any more trouble. There is not much chance of that these days. I am still smoking pot daily, as it numbs my nervousness, blunts my guilt, calms my thoughts, helps me sleep. I know it will not change anything. I will still lose my job, the frustrations of living with this virus will continue, Sean will stay a tainted memory. I should not be using pot as a coping mechanism. God should be that, but I have yet to really face Him.

But how can I not face Him? He created me, gave me everything, saved me, and set me apart for Him. How can I turn away from the only one who can give me everything I really need? No human can do that. No human has the power over every single cell in my body and soul. He is everything. So why did I get so riled up over a mere mortal man, and let my emotions for him drive me into insane thoughts and actions? What is it about me that just did not follow the leading of God? Do I not trust God?

Lack of Trust

"In God I trust and am not afraid.
What can man do to me?"
– Psalms 56:11

"Blessed is the one who trusts in the Lord,
who does not look to the proud,
to those who turn aside to false gods."
– Psalms 40:4

"Do not be wise in your own eyes;
fear the Lord and shun evil."
– Proverbs 3:7

"For I know the plans I have for you,
declares the Lord, plans to prosper you and not
to harm you, plans to give you a hope and a future."
– Jeremiah 29:11

"If any of you lacks wisdom, you should ask God,
who gives generously to all without finding fault,
and it will be given to you."
– James 1:5

"My only aim is to finish the race and complete
the task the Lord Jesus has given me."
– Acts 20:24

"We also know that the Son of God has come and has
given us understanding, so that we may know
Him who is true."
– 1 John 5:20

The Bible abounds with verses that direct us to trust in God's wisdom, not our own; to read His word and pray to discern what His will is. I have read and studied the Bible thoroughly, so I know the guidelines and truths. Yet I allow compromises to slip in, and then, I go my own way. I do trust that God is all-knowing, but I let that fallen nature slip into my life, and I start losing the race again. My spiritual life seems to parallel my physical running. I discipline myself to train and run regularly; then I laze away and get out of shape again, making starting over again all the more difficult. Tasks, work, laziness, and discouragement keep me from discipline in my running. So, also spiritual discipline is lacking. Consequently, I do not stay strong in either. My faith has never wavered and never will, but my discipline and trust do.

I have never really trusted many people in my life, especially men. I trusted my first husband as I knew him and his character. This indicates that to trust someone, we have to really know them. What follows that, then, is that to trust God, we need to know Him, and that we can do by studying His Word. I have done that, so I do trust that God knows what is best for me. But I still try to take the reins and rely on myself in certain situations. Does that mean that I do not really trust Him totally, or am I just letting the rebellious part of my human nature take over when it suits me?

Brighter Days

I had accepted the fact that my most-loved job was about to end when I got a call asking me if I'd like a casual, part-time position. Immediately, I said yes. My career there would not be over. I had accepted that I would have to go back to community nursing, even though I had sought to get a note to bar me from that during the virus. Alas, I decided to quit the agency altogether and just work part-time. I was tired of all the long hours and night shifts. I needed to settle into a calmer and less arduous life, hoping soon to be able to hug my grandchildren instead of seeing them from the approved distance.

The government announced that churches in my province could open again to 30 percent capacity with all the required regulations in place. I wondered how it would be determined who would be picked for that 30 percent. And would I now be able to face seeing Sean again? I was thinking, in my numb state, that I did not really care what he thought, and that it was no longer any of his business what I did or did not do. I would pretend he no longer existed for me. He could judge me inside his head all he wanted. (However, at times I wondered if he is almost glad of what I had done. I had given him a way out. He could stay content, feeling self-righteous and free of guilt for any of his wrongs or offenses.)

I have already found myself guilty, sentenced myself to shame, and locked up my heart where it belongs.

Hope?

"Why, my soul, are you downcast?
Why so disturbed within me? Put your hope in God,
for I will praise Him, my Savior and my God."
– Psalms 42:5

The psalms of David have, in the past, been a comfort and help to me. The boy David, the court musician David, and lastly, the king David certainly had his share of sorrow and joy. He was said to have a heart for God, but he failed at times in his life and often had to repent of his sinful deeds. I know God uses fallible people to be what we see as the *greats* of the Bible, so that we can relate more directly to their weakness and not feel as if we have to be perfect to be worthy of His love. We are to live in His strength, not our own. Using the fact of our weak humanity, however, does not give us an excuse to sin deliberately. But it shows that there is a way back if we do.

So, why have I not taken the way back? Why am I still sitting stuck at the side of the road? My heart is still feeling as deflated as a flat tire, my spiritual gas tank feels empty, and I feel too tired to make a call. But alas, I know that, like the CAA, help is only one call away.

I know I will not feel better or complete until I confess to God what he obviously already knows I did. But why can I not just do it? It's not complicated. I will not get struck by lightning. He will not refuse to forgive me. He knows I am sorry. I think it's the constant feeling that I do not deserve to be forgiven, since I should have been too wise to do what I did, or to think like I did. Knowing I cannot talk to anyone about what I did should make it a relief to talk to God about it.

But alas, here I am, still stuck.

Running Away

"I am the vine, you are the branches.
If you remain in Me and I in you, you will bear much
fruit; apart from Me you can do nothing."
– John 15:5

"Return to your rest, my soul,
for the Lord has been good to you."
– Psalms 116:7

I do not know if anyone really believes that they can run away or hide from God. To me, God is right there, closer than my own body to me. I have turned my back on Him a few times, but I knew He was right there next to me, waiting. I only had to turn around. We can run, but God always has us in His sight. The journey back can seem arduous and long, but in reality, it's shorter than a breath. I have always known this. It's that one step I needed to take.

I have cried out in the night to Him that I am sorry, lying in the dark with my thoughts, trying to find sleep. I have also cried out to Him about a condition I had gotten from overdoing. I did everything when I was married, everything for my husband. I worked full time, did all the childcare planning, had a spotless house, did all the yard work, took the kids to all their activities, took care of the family finances, went to aerobics, church, Bible study with its homework, all the vacation planning and prep, and even, for a few years, did the books for his business.

But why I mention this in passing is that it brought to mind that I might have also been over*doing* with Sean. Do, do, do. If I did enough, would he like me more? Was I too much a Martha and not enough a Mary?

I always thought of myself as a combination of Jesus's friends Martha and Mary. I have always been doing, trying to please, trying to gain approval. But somewhere in there, I had lost sight of who I really should have been trying the most to please: God. I thought I was doing all the things that I was supposed to. The one thing I see now, looking back at my whole life as a Christian, is that I was not trusting God enough. Nor His timing. Not waiting for His timing, I ran off and got lost in my impatient will.

Trying to run away from God's will is like a puppy running away from its mother. At first, it's all fun and freedom and frolic. But eventually, reality will set in and life alone, without its lifeline, has to be faced. The puppy might survive—it might even do pretty well—or end up tragically cold, alone, hungry, and afraid. But if he had made his way back to his mother, his nurturer, the one who knew what was best for him, the one who loved him, the one he could trust the most, life would be as it should be. Not that we are puppies or that our lives are simple. But why run away from the One who knows us best and wants to nurture us into a mature Christian? I've done my running, so there is no judging on my part. It is a trait of our human nature, thinking we can do it our way.

I have to stop running away; stop thinking I know what God's will is. I confessed my sins to God today and asked His forgiveness. I need, now, to listen to Him, follow His guidance—not my fallible mind's misguidance. I will have to wait on my decision regarding the group and church. Make no precipitous decisions on my own, decisions based on emotions or misguided ideas. Church is allowed to resume now—with restrictions, of course. I will wait and see.

God's will and ways are simple. It is we humans that complicate things.

Reflections

I have been writing this to reach some clarification in my mind as to why I do as I do, and why I made so many mistakes in the relationship with Sean. The *why* is simple. I was not seeking the will of God. I was not trusting God or His ways. I was compromising for selfish reasons. I could psychoanalyze my past and upbringing and experiences as precipitating factors, but that is only a partial and earthly way to get at the bad roots and the weeds in my life—the roots being the basic underlying causes, the weeds the bad things I let thrive.

I could bring up in my mind the image of my often-absent father, who never seemed to like my mother much. The image of a man who was rarely home and who left us when I was a teenager and died six months later, at a very young age. I know the relationship between a daughter and father is significant, but I never really had one. I idolized him over my hardworking mother, who I mistakenly thought to be unreasonable and undeserving. There, so began for me the ignoring of reality and excusing a man's neglectful behaviour. I never realized until after my mother died how hard she had had it and how my father leaving had not been her fault. I yearn for the day I get to Heaven to see her and apologize for all the wrong views that I had of her. However, I know that all the sorrows of the past are soon forgotten in eternity.

Incorrect thoughts can ingrain themselves in our minds. If we do not let God overrule these patterns of thinking, our minds can be ruled by misconceptions. These misconceptions could be followed by wrongful patterns of behaviour.

What I Should Have Seen

1. *Barring* being off to war or other urgent circumstances, if a man does not seem interested in seeing you too often, then he is just not interested in you, period. Wait for the next bus, ladies.

2. *If* a man seems to be lying to you, or just making up stuff, do not ignore it, thinking it does not matter. It does. Holding back the truth is akin to holding back genuine, God-like respect.

3. *If* a man does not want you to mention his name in any social media because he values his "privacy" so much, ask him why he has to keep your relationship so private.

4. *If* a man mentions things he wants to do with you, small or big, but never does them, then assume that he'd rather be doing them with someone else. Find someone who will do things with you.

5. *Never* assume because the man you are with is a Christian, that sex outside of marriage must be okay, since he is alright with it. God is quite plain about this. If you are worth it to him, he will wait.

6. *Never* discuss anything about the man you are dating with anyone, no matter how well-meaning it

may seem at the time. Their take on things will be different than yours. Plus, your or his past mistakes are just that: *past*.

7. *Do not* become so obsessed with finding the "truth" that you lose yourself or your rational thinking. Being with someone you do not trust is a slippery slope down into constant fussing, worrying, and anxiety. No one is worth that. And if the trust issues are just yours, consult the One you know you can always trust.

Waiting

"Wait for the Lord; be strong and take heart
and wait for the Lord."
– Psalms 27:14

"Be joyful in hope, patient in affliction,
faithful in prayer."
– Romans 12:12

*I*t has been three months and six days since my embarrassing and ridiculous behaviour. I have been to church twice, masked and sitting on the *x* spots. Sean was not there. I assumed he would not be, as he sometimes went to a different church, in the city. I was glad of that. Still a chicken; still hoping to avoid the inevitable. No singing allowed as yet, so no group practice. No having to see his face or trying to avoid looking at him at all. I still feel the sting of shame. It seems like it will never go away. I imagine scenarios in my mind where he has told the group about what I did and, consequently, I get told I am no longer welcome. A blunt email sent to remove the sinful stalker from the group. Oh, poor Sean, we did not know. We are so sorry for what she put you through. We must remove such a sick individual from our vicinity. We thought Liza was an okay person. Let us pray for your healing from such trauma.

But I should not put words or thoughts into people's minds. Especially not Christian ones. They are all wonderful human beings in the group, and not capable of real malice. But if what I did is not deserving of being banished from the group, it still leaves me with the question in my mind: should I just leave anyway? I still am unable to figure that out. I know God should be the one to give me direction, plus there may not be a group for months to come if this virus persists, along with its restrictions for gatherings. So, all I guess I can do now is wait.

My bestie once said I was the "roughy toughy of waiting it out." And that has been true in most of my relationships. I always waited and waited, often too long, to see if things would change. So, why was I so impatient with Sean? Was I not "roughy toughy" anymore? Or was I just tired of waiting for a man to treat me as if he really did love me—especially because he said that he did?

Did I expect too much from him? Was he not able to be in the kind of relationship that I wanted? Was I controlling? And the most important question: could I ever accept that it was all just a lie on his part from the start, and that he was just using me? I know I am asking questions that will never be answered. Do I need or want the answers, anyway?

I know I need the answers about myself. Also, I need the willingness to really look at myself with clear eyes—eyes that will see the truth about my own thoughts and actions.

As for Sean, it's time to give up. Time to let go. Time to let it be. Let go and let God take it from here.

Comfortable Solitude

As I lie in bed
Nothing worse can be said
Than what I say to myself
As I stay
In comfortable solitude.

No one fills the space
That was your place
So, I'm not thinking of you
While I stay
In comfortable solitude.

I would not look at those eyes
That had told many lies
As I'd rather stay alone
Truthfully
In comfortable solitude.

Feeling free of worry
I don't need to be sorry
That I would rather be alone
With myself
In comfortable solitude.

When my life meets its end
On God only I depend
To keep me in peace
Until I rest
In Heavenly solitude.

Disappointing God and Self

"Against You, You only, have I sinned and done
what is evil in Your sight; so, You are right in
Your verdict and justified when You judge."
– Psalms 51:4

"If we confess our sins, He is faithful
and just and will forgive us our sins and
purify us from all unrighteousness."
– 1 John 1:9

This earthly life is short in comparison to the eternity that comes after it. It's just a precursor to a better time, a dress rehearsal for the final act of passing to the other side, the preface to the real story—an earthly spiritual preparation for the heavenly and perfect union with God and Jesus.

So, in this vein of thinking, why did I not, at some point, especially after leaving the only real relationship in my life, say to myself *Whoa lady, stop. This is a temporary life. Seeking worldly pleasures is fruitless.* Why was it just so easy, at times, to stray away from God and all that I believed in? I have asked myself that very question so many times in my life. I still have not ascertained the true answer. Or maybe I am just avoiding the answer.

I could theorize that, in one period of my life, I was just rebelling against the emotional constrictions of my first marriage. But when we rebel, it is against God and His ways and protection. However, I do believe that He does still protect us, even in our sinful periods. I know that He allows us to suffer the earthly consequences of our sins. Some may feel that this is punishment, but with no consequences, no lessons will be learned.

The end of my second short and disastrous marriage did bring me closer to God. God had brought me to a point where I could finally see that He was all that I needed. Post-separation, I drew nearer to God, and He was my sustainer and strength. Another rebellion was not going to happen, and it did not. I was steadfast in my vow to stay away from the source of falling back into old patterns. Patterns that caused me to lose sight of what was right for me, and what was right in God's eyes.

But—along came Sean, who had so many of the qualities that I loved. Like those in my past, I picked a man, again, who was not emotionally available. Plus, not physically available very often as well.

But I will not blame him for my shameful behaviour. As I look back at our relationship, I feel sick, as I know I made so many mistakes that only I am responsible for. I cannot know how much I misconstrued about him, but I do know there is no misconstruing where I was wrong.

It's been a little over four months since that night I made a total fool of myself. I still cringe at my behaviour and look at myself with loathing. I wonder if I will ever get over the guilt of it; I wonder if I will ever feel like I am anywhere near normal. I look back and see that I was trying to construct a kind of relationship that suited my view of what it should be. All that stuff that I was doing to make him feel that I was wonderful and loving and desirable came to nothing. I wanted so much to impress him, but nothing I did impressed him at all. He even said he did not want to be impressed. I now believe I went overboard in trying to get him to see me as who he needed. Me, me, me . . . *ugh*. How not biblical.

I believe now that nothing I could have done would ever have impressed him. I also feel that he never really liked me or who I was. So, it appears to me that I had wasted my time trying to be loving, giving, affectionate, sexy, intelligent, spiritual. So, it comes down to questioning why he was even with me to begin with. Maybe I simply had been used. Certainly, there is nothing to be done about it now.

All I know for sure is that I will never again be in a relationship. I gave my all to him, confided my all to him, and still, it amounted to nothing to him. Yes, I am being morose. I feel like crying, but no tears will be wasted on this. I failed God and myself, because I set no boundaries. I just jumped into it full tilt, forgetting again to pull back and focus on what was real, focus on what I should have learned from my past mistakes, and what disappointment those mistakes brought.

There is nothing worse to me than disappointing people, but the ultimate is disappointing God. It would be interesting to know what that translates to in His mind when He sees us in the throes of ungodly behaviour. Maybe the acknowledgement on our parts and our sincere pleas for forgiveness obliterate how He sees our disappointing behaviour. He forgives us. He still loves us.

But thanks be to God, one day, I will leave this faulty, earthly body and mind. I so look forward to a glorified body and mind like Christ's, free of physical and emotional defects. And to be finally able to see clearly all that God only lets us see now with unclear, human eyes.

Oh My, Again!
Four Months and
Ten Days In

I went to an outdoor surprise birthday party last night during a visit to my bestie. I saw a young man there who looked so much like Sean that it astonished me. Same eyes, same facial expressions, same hands, same colouring, tall, slim. He just looked so much like Sean, I could not stop looking at him. I looked up Sean's profile on Facebook, thinking I would show it to my bestie to see what she thought of the comparison. But of course, I was still blocked by him. I felt a sinking feeling in my stomach, that feeling again of disgust for my past actions, that feeling you get when you know someone thinks that you are a stalking weirdo.

That's when I discovered I still had some kind of feelings for him. That I still cared what he thought of me. Ugh, a million times over. How could that be?

I was again questioning my returning to my church or the group. Again, I was starting to panic, saying things to myself like: *What should I do? Oh my gosh, what am I going to do? What if people know? Will someone say something? Do they know? What has he told his family, the church? Maybe I had better not go back, not risk any embarrassment. Hide.*

These thoughts were just taking me backward. I thought I had made progress. To myself, I said, *Stay calm. Remember that he is not good for you. Remember that you said you would leave the decision up to God. Remember that more time will pass before the group will be singing.*

But then, he is not going to forget what I did. I will have to see or feel his look of derision. His family will hate me, think I am a mental case.

Stop.

I even started to have a panic attack while we were out walking the dogs after leaving the party early. I told my bestie about the panic, but in no way could I tell her the real reason for it, my best friend of so many years. I went on about feeling overwhelmed in general—work, my new course, family worries, feeling so tired, feeling old, fed up with my weight gain and lack of exercise discipline. I felt like a liar, but it was too mortifying for me to talk about with her. I was truly disgusted with myself.

I mused over these feelings for some days after returning home. I wanted to cry, but I did not let myself. I did not deserve to let out the pent-up feelings still present. I did not deserve to feel any relief from my guilt. I could not forgive myself. I was still mortified. Ideas ran through my head as my mind made repeated, futile attempts to understand the brief relationship with Sean.

It entered my mind that perhaps I was overly vigilant for any sign that I was being deceived, like I had been in my brief, horrendous second marriage to—I have concluded—a psychopath. Maybe I was being needlessly suspicious, fearing I would let myself be fooled again by another disingenuous man. As a Christian, I know that I really need his forgiveness for anything I had falsely believed, but since I would never know what was false or true, God would have to take care of it—or show me how to deal with it.

Righteous Enough?

"The prayer of a righteous person is
powerful and effective."
– James 5:16

"The Lord is far from the wicked, but
He hears the prayer of the righteous."
– Proverbs 15:29

"Dear children, do not let anyone lead you astray.
The one who does what is right is righteous,
just as He is righteous."
– 1 John 3:7

"You see that a person is considered righteous
by what they do and not by faith alone."
– James 2:24

"For in the gospel, the righteousness of
God is revealed—a righteousness that is by faith
from first to last, just as it is written:
'The righteous will live by faith.'"
– Romans 1:17

"He saved us, not because of righteous things
we had done, but because of His mercy.
He saved us through the washing of rebirth
and renewal by the Holy Spirit."
– Titus 3:5

I was pondering last night, almost five months into this attempt at gaining introspection, at what it means to be righteous. As the verses above indicate, we are saved from our natural state of unrighteousness by our belief and faith in Christ and the salvation we receive from being reborn in Him and renewed by the Holy Spirit. The concept of being righteous came up in my mind as I was remembering Proverbs 15:9, a verse that says "He hears the prayer of the righteous." When I have sinned, I have a fear that God will not hear my prayers because I have not been righteous. Or that maybe that I am not righteous at all. That reeks of letting Satan into my ear to cause discouragement. Throughout my Christian life, that has been the thing that really affects me negatively. Plus, I have the thinking that I can never be righteous enough, as I fail too often. Since this failure with Sean and my subsequent abhorrent behaviour, I have let the discouragement in again. I know God has forgiven me, as I have confessed my sins to Him, but my lack of self-forgiveness is preventing me from moving away from the shame of it all.

Self-forgiveness has always been difficult for me. Tending to be a bit of a perfectionist and a lover of resolution likely does not help. I need to talk to God; I need to ask for His help in this. I know this, but I do not do it. Therein comes that thought again: am I righteous enough to ask God? Is there a scale to measure righteousness? Well, of course not, so why does the thought even enter my head? Obviously, I should know that only God and Jesus are truly righteous, and that any righteousness we have is through them. It is seen in us only through their eyes. It is only their righteousness that is the measurement of ours. So, read the Word, woman, *read*. Even if you have heard and read the verses many times over, read them again.

" And humbly accept the Word
planted in you, which can save you."
– James 1:2

"For the Word of God is alive and active.
Sharper than any double-edged sword, it penetrates
even to dividing soul and spirit, joint and marrow;
it judges the thoughts and attitudes of the heart."
– Hebrews 4:12

"All Scripture is God-breathed and is useful
for teaching, rebuking, correcting, and
training in righteousness."
– 2 Timothy 3:16

I have been writing in a journal since the beginning of the year, making comments on scripture I have looked up on various words or subjects. I gained insight with reading and meditating, but often, I can see, when rereading my journal, that I have not followed through on what I discerned at the time of the journalling. I had written: *In the above with Sean, I must not lose myself again; yet still not demand more than he is able to give.* Well, I failed on both of those. Goes to show the reason God wants us to stay in the Word is that repetition can be a constant reminder of what we are to be thinking and doing. The verse I had not thought of here was, from Philippians 2:3–4, "Do nothing out of selfish ambition or vain conceit. Rather, in humility, value others above yourselves, not looking to your own interests but each of you to the interests of others."

Memorizing scripture would be better, as His Word would be permanently accessible at the moment I needed it. And I had those moments.

In February, I had written: *I could never explain how Christ looks at us, but I know that I must change how I see myself. I cannot hate myself and at the same time be Christlike, as Christ had no hatred in Him. Is it possible to look at myself with love?* A reminder to be more Christlike comes from a verse in Romans 12 that says we are to "be transformed by the renewing of our minds." Many places in scripture also tell us to love our neighbours as we love ourselves. It takes a lot of striving for me to love myself right now.

Later in February: *If my mind is to be free from enslavement to negative thoughts and thoughts that result in wrong actions and reactions, I need to keep my mind on what*

God has given me to think on—His salvation, His truth, His love, His grace. If I dwell on my Heavenly future and not on the temporary cares of this world, my mind will find peace and not the anxiety this world has to offer me. As Colossians 3:2 says, "Set your minds on things above, not on earthly things."

Late in March, a few weeks into COVID restrictions, I wrote: *Right now, we need each other more than ever. We need to be strong in the Lord, strong toward each other, and strong in our willingness to stop remaining in our complaining about this changed world we are presently living in Joshua 1:9 says, "Be strong and courageous. Do not be afraid; do not be discouraged, for the Lord your God will be with you wherever you go." The world needs God more than ever right now, with so many sick, so much uncertainty and fear, chaos from riots and violent protests, and weather on Earth seeming out of control. With many churches closed or with limited services and attendance, we are missing fellowship with other believers when we really need it.*

Many more things were written in my journal, but I will jump forward into what I was seeking to find out about early one September, and most of my adult Christian life. How do I know what God's will is for me? Number one, I need to be still. As Psalms 46:10 says, "Be still and know that I am God." Being still is very difficult for me, as my mind wanders or gets fixated on tasks. In not being still, I am not listening to what God is saying to me. Right now, I am trying to be still and ascertain what God wants me to do about returning to the church group after things are back to normal.

The book of James says we are to ask God for wisdom and believe that He will give it to us. But it will be God's wisdom, not ours. James 3:17 says, "But the wisdom that comes from Heaven is first of all pure, then peace-loving, considerate, submissive, full of mercy and good fruit, impartial, and sincere."

So, with this verse in mind, should I ask myself some questions? Would it be "impure" to go back to my church? No. Would it be "peace-loving"? Only if my presence did not cause a disturbance to anyone. That is an unpredictable one, as I cannot know Sean's thoughts or his family's. Would returning be "considerate"? Maybe to the leader of the group who wants me back to assist in worship music. "Good fruit"—might that not indicate to me that stopping attending church, and thus not taking my beloved granddaughter with me, would be spiritually detrimental to her in the long run? "Impartial"—that is, considering myself no more important than anyone else? "Sincere"—am I sincere in my motives for returning? They cannot be self-serving. And the hardest one: "submissive"—am I willing to be submissive to the will of God in this matter, even if it means I experience feeling self-conscious, humiliated, and a fool?

Jesus suffered; therefore, so should I. I will continue to wait on the Lord.

Nothing

There is no end to something
That never really happened
It began but died
Before it lived.

I imagined there was love
From a heart made of stone
But my love shattered
As it touched yours.

You played the part of lover
In a game I could not win
I could only lose
Everything and you.

Hiding yourself was clever
So, nothing was ever real
Leaving me no choice
But to guess who you were.

I will now forget your face
So false with lying eyes
For the truth now is,
We did not exist.

Self-Importance

"Do not merely listen to the Word,
and so deceive yourselves. Do what it says."
– James 1:22

*W*ere all the things that I did for Sean, or wanted from Sean, out of selfishness? Was I placing my needs above his? Did I assume I knew what his needs were?

It's hard to admit to being selfish. I often think I am not selfish, but do admit to being too self-centred. We are all born self-centred, of course, with the curse of being human and prone to our selfish ways. I had thought that I was doing all the right things for Sean, but in retrospect, I can see I was being a bit overbearing and perhaps trying to have things go the way that I thought they should. Not that he was innocent. He was selfish with his time, vague with details, and insistent on his terms. But in the end, I have to get it through my head that none of that matters now. I need to hear what God is wanting me to learn from this failed relationship.

I know that I have learned that I have been a failure at relationships with men and need to stay away from them. I have subsequently decided that I will not pursue any relationships again. Being blessed with a full and busy life, along with many present family obligations, has to be enough. I am older and need to concentrate on my eternal future, not some relationship that would only be a temporary thing. It's not easy admitting to myself that I am a screwup, but it would be worse repeating a failure with its subsequent shame.

I never wanted to be a divorced person, always having wanted a marriage that lasted into old age and eternity. Looking back, I can see that I should have had more faith and trust in God to stay with my first husband. Regret can be futile, and perhaps I needed the lessons that I have learned since then. God allows us to do what we want, and I am thankful that He has stayed beside me during all my mistakes. He has let me learn my lessons the hard way.

If Jesus Came to Visit

I was thinking last night, if Jesus came to visit your or my home today, would we feel any shame or guilt? I do not mean if the dishes were not done, the kids were fighting, the place was a mess, or dust was collected on our Bibles. Jesus knows all we think, say, and do already, so would we have shame in any of those areas while in His presence? But, what would we say? What would we talk about? Or could we even talk at all? What would we say if He asked, "What have you done today to further My kingdom?" Or, "What have you done for the needy or sorrowful?" I know I would feel like bowing down on the floor with hesitation before I could look into His pure, loving eyes. I had a dream many years ago in which Jesus was at my house. I cannot fully describe His eyes, as I just tried to. There is no human word that would suffice as to what they looked like.

I know that Jesus has already died for my sins, even my recent ones. When confessed, they are already forgiven. But still, in His direct presence, I think I'd feel that I would have nothing to say. Just looking into His eyes would be enough.

But we are always in the presence of Jesus and God, whether They come to our front door or not. We always have access to Them; They know us more than any living being. Their constant love should make me think about all my time-wasting and woe-is-me thinking. But the curse of still being in earthly form continues.

Small Victories

"My sheep listen to my voice;
I know them, and they follow Me."
– John 10:27

"But thanks be to God!
He gives us the victory through
our Lord Jesus Christ."
– 1Corinthians 15:57

*I*t has been a little over six months since my embarrassing and ridiculous behaviour, and still the guilt remains. I still think about Sean, all the mistakes that I made, and how I still feel mortified that I was so stupid. Not a nice word, but the correct word.

But I have had one small victory on the man front. The old male acquaintance I was briefly seeing texted me after a time of no contact, and I could tell he was hinting at starting a sexual relationship. Kind out of the blue, but quite obvious. And I will not lie, I was tempted. But I knew that to fall back into old ways was not the way I should go. I told him about my faith and beliefs. He tried to change my mind. I plainly told him I was not interested in a serious or sexual relationship. Have not heard from him since. *Men!* And yay for me!

Even if victories are small, I think we need them. Small victories to some can be big victories to others. And as we build on them, we get stronger in our faith and more prepared to win another victory.

Any victories that I have had or strength that I now have to get through the many stresses I have in my life come only from God. They are certainly not from me. Yes, at times, I do cry out to God, "I cannot take this anymore!" Yet He knows in His strength that I will. In some ways, I am an impatient person, so waiting on God is difficult for me, but I know He sees it all, and I must wait on Him.

Waiting, Lord. Impatiently, but waiting.

Comedy Act

I was lying in bed last night and trying to turn my brain off, but these somewhat funny things kept coming to my mind. Here is how it went. It was me, in my mind, trying to do a comedy act:

I am from Canada, and I love Canada and its people. We are polite than, you know . . . that little country to the south of us. I must admit that I like that they have what is called Social Security. What we have is . . . *Old Age Security pension*. Why did they have to call it that? Why not *over-a-certain-age* pension? Or *glad-you-made-it-this-far-to-collect-our-free-money* pension? *Ugh*, I mumble into my sleeve when asked what extra pension money I receive.

But then, I have to think—one day older is one day closer to Heaven. In Heaven, I will not look old anymore. I'll look thirty, perfect. But then, maybe it will not matter what we look like, just as long as we are there. Maybe we will look like what I imagine Moses looked like. Long white hair, long white beard, nice strong handmade leather sandals and a long, flowing robe. And don't forget that staff.

But what about that robe? Was it woolly and itchy? I imagine him standing at the edge of the Red Sea, the Israelites behind him and the Egyptians close on their heels. Moses says to God, "Can I just take five?" Moses takes off his robe, but not the undergarments, as no skinny-dipping was allowed. He jumps into the Red Sea, but forgets he cannot swim (or how deep the water can get). God shakes His head "I knew it!" (Of course He did). God parts the Red Sea and Moses sinks to dry land, cooled off but mortified. The Hebrew leaders run to his aid, with his long, itchy robe in hand. Seeing the leaders and Moses running, everyone else starts to run or walk, and the nation of God is crossing the Red Sea. I know that's not exactly how the crossing started, but something had to give them a nudge. Those in the very back row wonder why they have to be in the back as small drops of water touch their calves and they hear the Egyptians closing in. Will they be caught? Why do they have to be the last in line?

But, people of God, no one is in the back. Jesus is right behind you, protecting you on all sides. Some people will take longer to get there. Do not look back, and never give up. Keep running.

I think of them wandering in the same desert for forty years, most of them having been born in that wilderness, and a lot dying there, too. Childbirth must have been a real hoot. They whined about the accommodations. They whined about the food. They whined about the heat and sand. They had God travelling with them and an emissary with direct communication between them and the Big Guy. They even had a set of concrete rules, set in stone. Sounds like things never change. We have McD and they had McManna. They had meat fall from the sky, and we can eat out or take out. We have the Bible and direct access to God. But we still complain. History never stops repeating itself.

And that time when Moses lost his temper and smacked that rock. Sadly, he got banned from the Promised Land for doing that. Oh my. Glad that does not happen to us every time we lose our temper. I'd be in the pit with Joseph by now—maybe dressed in my own nifty outfit, like his coat of many colours—but in the pit, anyway.

And then the golden calf? Moses is gone longer than they wanted, so they throw all of their jewelry that they had hidden for years from the enemy into a pot and made a calf to worship. Surely, this one golden thing would save them all from their boredom. Look how cute he was to them! Impatient, they were. Not like us, eh? *Yeah, right.* We live in an instantaneous society. No waiting for us. We surely are waiting now, during this pandemic. It makes me wonder if we could have survived the aftermath of the golden calf—having to drink the melted-down gold, suffer the violent death of some of the rebels, and endure the plagues of punishment afterward. Sounds rough to me. I wonder why we are not struck by lightning, as we are no different than those who struggled in that personally-designed-for-the-Israelites desert.

I think we all must know how difficult it was for them in the desert. Sand in everything. Always hot and dry. Those awful sandstorms. Same food, day after day. Crying babies and whiny kids. The old getting older faster. How tired do we get if our walk is just a little bit longer than we had wanted? They walked for forty years, and most got nowhere. Sounds like treadmill walking. We all have our deserts.

And bibbity-bobbity, that staff of Moses's. It was described as the staff of God—no fairy godmother wand, folks. This had real Godly power to it. No three genie wishes; no magic carpet, either. The staff of God. With it, Moses started the plagues on Egypt; he made water come out of a rock; then snakes—*yuck, snakes.* The Hebrew nation was whining again, so they got bitten by snakes sent from God. Lots of snakes in our present world, but they are sent by the biggest snake of all. We just have to resist, as we have grace and faith. The poor Israelites had to get bitten, suffer, believe, and then have faith that looking up at the bronze snake, as they were directed, would cure them of the poison in their bodies and souls. *Hey, wait*—that sounds a bit similar to us! We get bitten by that snake of old Satan, who poisons us, but if we believe and look up to Christ on the cross (His staff of power given from Him to us), we are saved by grace from the venom of sin. I love the parallels in the Bible found between the Old and New Testaments.

Just a real reminder that we will all, in faith, get out of our deserts and end up in our promised land, Heaven. Don't you just want to give Moses a big, long hug? And maybe a new pair of Birks?

I need to stop my mind wandering around in the desert of Sean. Put my new sandals on and get to the oasis of self-forgiveness and peace.

Addiction

Drip, drip
Take a sip
Try a puff
Only one pill
Drip, drip
It's coming now.

Drip, drip
Drink some more
Inhale it deeper
Let's try two
Drip, drip
It's coming quicker.

Drip, drip
Cannot get enough
My lungs want the fire
Higher is better
Drip, drip
You are going faster.

Drip, drip
My body is poisoned
The cancer has spread
My craving is killing me
Drip, drip
Slowly, all are going.

Drip, drip
The throat no more can swallow

The lungs no more can breathe
The heart no more can beat
Drip, drip
Slowly, all are gone.

Drip, drip
The mother's tears will flow
The daughter's fears won't end
The sisters' grief remains
Drip, drip
Chances are no more.

Drip, drip
Like rain, the cycle starts
The child repeats again
The pain returns to life
Drip, drip
God cries.

Drip, drip
Blood comes off the thorns
Forgiveness bought for all
Drip, drip
Jesus is Freedom.

Not Loving

Just say that you love me
Just say that you don't
Just break my heart now
Or say that you won't
Give me a reason
To think that you will
For I'm all alone here
Loving you still.

I don't want to hear, I don't want to see
I don't want to feel you not loving me.

I do not know why these poems come to me, usually late at night, out of the blue. It has been seven months now to the day that I lost my mind and acted like an idiot. Still, I cannot get the mortifying guilt out of my head. Lately, life has become too much, too filled with stress and uncontrollable situations. I have not done any writing for the past two-and-a-half months, but I am enjoying a course, so that's a good stress. The rest, well, it is tirelessly complicated.

It is difficult to write all the details of the situations that are causing me, at this moment, to be depressed. But I will mention one thing.

My ex-husband died last week, and I was treated like a pariah by his present wife. I felt negated, like my twenty-eight years with him had been nothing. She only knows me by the appalling lies that he told her and many others about me. He was not a Christian when he was with me, and was verbally abusive toward me about my faith. At some point, he started going to church, and at the funeral, which I could only watch online, his faith and love for Jesus was the centre of his eulogy. Having missed a sharing of faith when I was with him affected me deeply. But with the wisdom that is hers, my daughter said that maybe if we had not split up, he might never have been saved. Only God knows. And I had to realize, deep in my heart, that no one could take away the time that I had had with him. I put two pictures of he and I together when we were first married on my dresser as a reminder that we had existed.

Knowing that I cannot undo the past does not make me feel any better. Would I go back if I could? Maybe. Anyone have a time machine?

There are other minor issues related to this earthly life, but have I forgotten that Jesus said we were not to worry? I know God will work things out, and I know that God has always gotten me through stress and strife.

My son is not coping well with losing his father. He cries and says he'd rather have him back as the mean person he was before than have nothing of him. I try to convince him that his father is in Heaven, out of his pain, and that in Heaven, we all get to know fully the real truth of things. All has changed for his father; it's not life as before. But he cannot grasp this.

I am just tired. I want peace—the peace that passes all understanding. Please, God.

Clearing the Conscience

"How much more, then, will the blood of Christ, who, through the eternal Spirit, offered Himself unblemished to God, cleanse our consciences from acts that lead to death, so that we may serve the living God?"
– Hebrews 9:14

"Let us draw near to God with a sincere heart and with the full assurance that faith brings, having our hearts sprinkled to cleanse us from a guilty conscience and having our bodies washed with pure water."
– Hebrews 10:22

"This is how we know that we belong to the truth and how we set our hearts at rest in His presence: If our heart condemns us, we know that God is greater than our hearts, and He knows everything."
– 1 John 3:19–20

I doubt anyone ever thinks of what I did eight months ago—but of course, I do. It never leaves my mind. It stays there like a toy train, going around and around on a circular toy track; the same incessant around-and-around-we-go. When it will stop, only God knows. Or, at times, I think it's like a thick, dark cloud hanging over my brain, refusing to leave. I know, I should let the breeze of sense just blow it softly away. Either way, the train needs to be derailed and the dark cloud dissipated. Why have I not done it? Why will I not let go of it? Could it be because I will not let go of Sean? Scary thought. Or is it because I cannot let go of caring what he thinks of me? It is useless to care what people think of you, as that is totally out of your own control.

The reason why I have been writing this has been to give myself insight as to why I do as I do, or why I did as I did. One conclusion I have come to is that I do not know how to have a relationship without becoming obsessed. Yes, that word again. To reason why I became this way seems a waste of time at this point in my life. And believing this, I have decided, with God's guidance, that the wisest choice is never to get into a relationship again. I am older. I am tired. I am no longer willing to become a person I cannot understand.

Reading the Bible verses above, I know that I must let go, get off the train, and let the sun (Son) melt the dark cloud away forever.

Bygones

A lot of time has gone by. I am no longer smoking pot. My mind is calm and my heart no longer aches. During almost one year of this pandemic, I hope that others have also discovered what really are the most important things in their lives. I know, once this mess is over, I want most to pick up my two young grandsons and hug them so tight. Not touching them for ten months now has been so frustrating, but protection is the key right now. Next, I want to hug everyone in my family without fear of germs, visit my bestie, and go to see my sister in another province and that new great-nephew of mine. And church, and singing. The simple things in life are the most important.

Christmas was sad, and empty of most family traditions. But it was only one Christmas. We can pray that the next will be filled with the things we missed this past one. We mourn those who lost their lives, praise God for those who were healed or spared, always remembering those who worked so hard in the worst of circumstances.

I can thank God for blessings during this pandemic. I still could work at the job I love, I remained healthy, I passed my course, I had time to consider that the insights I gained from this memoir were lessons from God.

No, I have not turned into the mature Christian that I should be, but I am working on it. I do think that it has taken me way too long, but some of us are just like that.

As for Sean, I think I am done with my shame. He was just a man, I am just a woman. I made mistakes, but God has forgiven me, and now I feel I can forgive myself. Dwelling in the past ruins the future. I pray he finds someone who can love him and be the partner he needs. As for me—it's just me and Jesus.

> "The name of the Lord is a strong tower.
> The righteous run into it and are safe."
> – Proverbs 18:20

> "Trust in the Lord with all your heart and lean not
> unto your own understanding; in all your ways submit
> to Him, and He will make your paths straight."
> – Proverbs 3:5–6

Please, mind your heart.

Missed Beats

My memories of you
Are faded
Vague
And uncertain.
Your perfect face
Now imperfect
Again.
I have no dreams
Or wonder
If you have
Any memory of me.
How can something
That was thought of
As love
Now be
Nothing
But missed beats
Of cold hearts.

Epilogue

*I*t has been some time since I have written anything. The virus is basically over. Church has fully resumed, but with no singing group. It has been dismantled, as some members did not return to our church—Sean being one of them. Life is almost normal for most—but not for me.

One sunny Sunday morning this past summer, after a night shift, I came home to find my son gone from this earth.

In life, we often think, in a particular moment, that it is the worst day of our lives. But it often is not. That was the worst day of my life. That was the day my heart really did break. That was the day nothing—*nothing*—else mattered to me. No past pain or behaviour meant anything. No relationship loss meant anything. No loss could compare to losing my son. I loved him so much.

That day was total devastation, total pain, total grief. There are not enough tears that can be shed; except maybe the tears of joy when I see him again.

My son had thought he would take all his pain with him when he left. But there is still pain left behind—the pain of losing him, of missing him. I will gladly keep that pain until I leave mine all behind, when I join him in Heaven.

God has sustained me. He has upheld me as only He can.

Perspective.

Printed in the USA
CPSIA information can be obtained
at www.ICGtesting.com
LVHW091559060124
768257LV00001B/82